50 Breakfast in Bed Recipes for Home

By: Kelly Johnson

Table of Contents

- Classic Buttermilk Pancakes
- Blueberry Lemon Ricotta Pancakes
- Fluffy Belgian Waffles with Maple Syrup
- French Toast with Cinnamon & Honey
- Croissant Breakfast Sandwich with Ham & Cheese
- Eggs Benedict with Hollandaise Sauce
- Smoked Salmon & Cream Cheese Bagel
- Avocado Toast with Poached Egg
- Nutella & Strawberry Crepes
- Classic Omelet with Cheese & Herbs
- Spinach & Feta Scrambled Eggs
- Overnight Oats with Chia Seeds & Berries
- Classic English Breakfast
- Breakfast Burrito with Sausage & Egg
- Fresh Fruit & Yogurt Parfait
- Cheddar & Bacon Breakfast Biscuits
- Banana Bread French Toast
- Cinnamon Roll Pancakes
- Chorizo & Egg Breakfast Tacos
- Flaky Almond Croissants
- Strawberry Shortcake Scones
- Baked Oatmeal with Apples & Walnuts
- Maple Pecan Sticky Buns
- Breakfast Quesadilla with Eggs & Salsa
- Eggs Florentine with Spinach & Hollandaise
- Peaches & Cream Waffles
- Biscuits & Country Sausage Gravy
- Hash Brown & Egg Skillet
- Caramelized Banana Oatmeal
- Creamy Polenta with Poached Eggs
- Savory Breakfast Galette with Mushrooms & Goat Cheese
- Classic Breakfast Muffins with Blueberries
- Peanut Butter & Banana Smoothie Bowl
- Sweet Potato & Black Bean Breakfast Hash
- Apple Cinnamon Crepes

- Pumpkin Spice Pancakes
- Sourdough Toast with Honey & Ricotta
- Soft-Boiled Eggs with Toast Soldiers
- Croque Madame with Gruyère & Ham
- Raspberry Almond Danish Pastries
- Green Smoothie Bowl with Granola
- Classic Breakfast Quiche with Bacon & Spinach
- Granola & Greek Yogurt with Honey
- Chocolate Chip Muffins with Espresso
- Coconut Chia Pudding with Mango
- Carrot Cake Waffles with Cream Cheese Drizzle
- Vanilla Bean Porridge with Roasted Nuts
- Cheesy Grits with Butter & Shrimp
- Mocha Smoothie with Almond Butter
- Freshly Baked Pain au Chocolat

Classic Buttermilk Pancakes

Ingredients:

- 1 1/2 cups all-purpose flour
- 2 tbsp sugar
- 1 tsp baking powder
- 1/2 tsp baking soda
- 1/2 tsp salt
- 1 1/4 cups buttermilk
- 1 egg
- 2 tbsp melted butter
- 1 tsp vanilla extract

Instructions:

1. Whisk together dry ingredients.
2. In a separate bowl, mix buttermilk, egg, melted butter, and vanilla.
3. Combine wet and dry ingredients (do not overmix).
4. Cook on a greased skillet over medium heat until golden brown on both sides.

Blueberry Lemon Ricotta Pancakes

Ingredients:

- 1 1/2 cups all-purpose flour
- 1 tsp baking powder
- 1/2 tsp baking soda
- 1/4 tsp salt
- 1/4 cup sugar
- 3/4 cup ricotta cheese
- 3/4 cup milk
- 2 eggs
- 1 tbsp lemon zest
- 1/2 cup fresh blueberries

Instructions:

1. Mix dry ingredients.
2. In a separate bowl, mix ricotta, milk, eggs, and lemon zest.
3. Combine wet and dry ingredients, then fold in blueberries.
4. Cook on a skillet over medium heat until golden brown.

Fluffy Belgian Waffles with Maple Syrup

Ingredients:

- 2 cups all-purpose flour
- 1 tbsp sugar
- 1 tbsp baking powder
- 1/2 tsp salt
- 2 eggs, separated
- 1 3/4 cups milk
- 1/2 cup melted butter
- 1 tsp vanilla extract

Instructions:

1. Whisk together dry ingredients.
2. In a separate bowl, mix egg yolks, milk, butter, and vanilla.
3. Beat egg whites until stiff peaks form and fold into batter.
4. Cook in a preheated waffle iron until golden brown.

French Toast with Cinnamon & Honey

Ingredients:

- 4 slices thick-cut bread
- 2 eggs
- 1/2 cup milk
- 1 tsp cinnamon
- 1 tsp vanilla extract
- 1 tbsp honey
- Butter for cooking

Instructions:

1. Whisk eggs, milk, cinnamon, vanilla, and honey.
2. Dip bread into mixture, coating both sides.
3. Cook in a buttered skillet over medium heat until golden brown.

Croissant Breakfast Sandwich with Ham & Cheese

Ingredients:

- 2 croissants, halved
- 4 slices ham
- 2 slices Swiss or cheddar cheese
- 2 eggs, scrambled
- 1 tbsp butter

Instructions:

1. Scramble eggs with butter.
2. Assemble croissants with ham, cheese, and scrambled eggs.
3. Toast in a pan or oven until cheese melts.

Eggs Benedict with Hollandaise Sauce

Ingredients:

- 2 English muffins, halved and toasted
- 4 slices Canadian bacon
- 4 poached eggs

Hollandaise Sauce:

- 3 egg yolks
- 1/2 cup unsalted butter, melted
- 1 tbsp lemon juice
- Salt and cayenne pepper to taste

Instructions:

1. Poach eggs in simmering water.
2. Cook Canadian bacon until browned.
3. Blend egg yolks, lemon juice, and melted butter to make hollandaise.
4. Assemble muffins with bacon, poached eggs, and hollandaise sauce.

Smoked Salmon & Cream Cheese Bagel

Ingredients:

- 2 bagels, halved and toasted
- 4 tbsp cream cheese
- 4 oz smoked salmon
- 1 tbsp capers
- 1/4 small red onion, thinly sliced

Instructions:

1. Spread cream cheese on toasted bagels.
2. Top with smoked salmon, capers, and red onion slices.

Avocado Toast with Poached Egg

Ingredients:

- 2 slices sourdough bread, toasted
- 1 ripe avocado, mashed
- 2 poached eggs
- 1/2 tsp red pepper flakes
- 1/2 tsp lemon juice
- Salt and black pepper, to taste

Instructions:

1. Spread avocado on toast and season with lemon juice.
2. Top with poached eggs and red pepper flakes.

Nutella & Strawberry Crêpes

Ingredients:

- 1 cup all-purpose flour
- 1 1/4 cups milk
- 2 eggs
- 1 tbsp sugar
- 1 tsp vanilla extract
- 1 tbsp butter, melted
- 1/2 cup Nutella
- 1/2 cup sliced strawberries

Instructions:

1. Blend all crepe ingredients (except Nutella and strawberries).
2. Cook thin crepes in a buttered pan.
3. Spread Nutella on crepes and top with strawberries.
4. Fold and serve warm.

Classic Omelet with Cheese & Herbs

Ingredients:

- 3 eggs
- 2 tbsp milk
- 1/4 cup shredded cheddar or Swiss cheese
- 1 tbsp butter
- 1 tbsp fresh herbs (chives, parsley, or dill), chopped
- Salt and pepper, to taste

Instructions:

1. Whisk eggs, milk, salt, and pepper.
2. Heat butter in a nonstick pan over medium heat.
3. Pour in eggs and cook, lifting edges to let uncooked eggs flow underneath.
4. Sprinkle cheese and herbs, fold, and serve.

Spinach & Feta Scrambled Eggs

Ingredients:

- 3 eggs
- 1/4 cup fresh spinach, chopped
- 1/4 cup crumbled feta cheese
- 1 tbsp butter
- Salt and black pepper, to taste

Instructions:

1. Sauté spinach in butter until wilted.
2. Add beaten eggs, cook until softly scrambled.
3. Stir in feta, season, and serve.

Overnight Oats with Chia Seeds & Berries

Ingredients:

- 1/2 cup rolled oats
- 1 tbsp chia seeds
- 1/2 cup milk or almond milk
- 1/2 cup mixed berries
- 1 tsp honey or maple syrup

Instructions:

1. Combine all ingredients in a jar.
2. Refrigerate overnight.
3. Stir before serving.

Classic English Breakfast

Ingredients:

- 2 eggs, fried or scrambled
- 2 sausages
- 2 slices bacon
- 1/2 cup baked beans
- 1 grilled tomato, halved
- 1 slice toast
- 1/2 cup sautéed mushrooms

Instructions:

1. Cook bacon and sausages.
2. Heat baked beans and sauté mushrooms.
3. Fry eggs and grill tomatoes.
4. Serve everything with toast.

Breakfast Burrito with Sausage & Egg

Ingredients:

- 2 large eggs
- 1 breakfast sausage, crumbled
- 1/4 cup shredded cheese
- 1 flour tortilla
- 1 tbsp salsa

Instructions:

1. Cook sausage in a pan.
2. Scramble eggs with sausage.
3. Fill tortilla with eggs, sausage, cheese, and salsa.
4. Wrap and serve.

Fresh Fruit & Yogurt Parfait

Ingredients:

- 1 cup Greek yogurt
- 1/2 cup granola
- 1/2 cup mixed berries
- 1 tbsp honey

Instructions:

1. Layer yogurt, granola, and berries in a glass.
2. Drizzle with honey.

Cheddar & Bacon Breakfast Biscuits

Ingredients:

- 2 cups all-purpose flour
- 1 tbsp baking powder
- 1/2 tsp salt
- 1/2 cup cold butter, cubed
- 1/2 cup shredded cheddar cheese
- 1/4 cup cooked bacon, crumbled
- 3/4 cup milk

Instructions:

1. Mix dry ingredients, then cut in butter.
2. Stir in cheese, bacon, and milk.
3. Bake at **400°F (200°C) for 12-15 minutes**.

Banana Bread French Toast

Ingredients:

- 4 slices banana bread
- 2 eggs
- 1/2 cup milk
- 1 tsp vanilla extract
- 1/2 tsp cinnamon
- 1 tbsp butter

Instructions:

1. Whisk eggs, milk, vanilla, and cinnamon.
2. Dip banana bread in mixture and cook in butter until golden.

Cinnamon Roll Pancakes

Ingredients:

- 1 cup pancake batter
- 1/4 cup brown sugar
- 1 tbsp cinnamon
- 1 tbsp melted butter

Cream Cheese Drizzle:

- 2 tbsp cream cheese
- 1 tbsp milk
- 1 tbsp powdered sugar

Instructions:

1. Mix brown sugar, cinnamon, and butter for a swirl.
2. Pour pancake batter into pan, swirl in cinnamon mix.
3. Cook and drizzle with cream cheese glaze.

Chorizo & Egg Breakfast Tacos

Ingredients:

- 2 eggs, scrambled
- 1/2 cup cooked chorizo
- 2 small tortillas
- 1 tbsp salsa
- 1 tbsp fresh cilantro

Instructions:

1. Scramble eggs with cooked chorizo.
2. Serve in tortillas with salsa and cilantro.

Flaky Almond Croissants

Ingredients:

- 4 day-old croissants
- 1/2 cup almond flour
- 1/4 cup powdered sugar
- 1/4 cup unsalted butter, softened
- 1 egg
- 1/2 tsp almond extract
- 1/4 cup sliced almonds
- Powdered sugar, for dusting

Instructions:

1. Preheat oven to **350°F (175°C)**.
2. Mix almond flour, powdered sugar, butter, egg, and almond extract into a paste.
3. Slice croissants open and spread almond paste inside.
4. Close croissants, spread a thin layer of paste on top, and sprinkle with sliced almonds.
5. Bake for **10-12 minutes** until golden brown.
6. Dust with powdered sugar before serving.

Strawberry Shortcake Scones

Ingredients:

- 2 cups all-purpose flour
- 1/4 cup sugar
- 1 tbsp baking powder
- 1/2 tsp salt
- 1/2 cup cold butter, cubed
- 1/2 cup heavy cream
- 1 egg
- 1 tsp vanilla extract
- 1 cup fresh strawberries, chopped

Instructions:

1. Preheat oven to **400°F (200°C)**.
2. Mix flour, sugar, baking powder, and salt.
3. Cut in cold butter until mixture resembles coarse crumbs.
4. Stir in cream, egg, and vanilla until just combined, then fold in strawberries.
5. Shape dough into a circle, cut into wedges, and place on a baking sheet.
6. Bake for **15-18 minutes** until golden brown.

Baked Oatmeal with Apples & Walnuts

Ingredients:

- 2 cups rolled oats
- 1/2 cup chopped walnuts
- 1/2 cup diced apples
- 1/4 cup brown sugar
- 1 tsp cinnamon
- 1/2 tsp baking powder
- 1/4 tsp salt
- 1 1/2 cups milk
- 2 eggs
- 1 tsp vanilla extract

Instructions:

1. Preheat oven to **375°F (190°C)**.
2. Mix oats, walnuts, apples, brown sugar, cinnamon, baking powder, and salt.
3. In another bowl, whisk milk, eggs, and vanilla, then combine with oat mixture.
4. Pour into a greased baking dish and bake for **30-35 minutes**.

Maple Pecan Sticky Buns

Ingredients:

- 1 sheet puff pastry or homemade dough
- 1/2 cup brown sugar
- 1/4 cup maple syrup
- 1/2 tsp cinnamon
- 1/4 cup chopped pecans
- 2 tbsp butter, melted

Instructions:

1. Preheat oven to **375°F (190°C)**.
2. Mix brown sugar, maple syrup, cinnamon, and pecans.
3. Roll out dough, spread mixture evenly, then roll into a log.
4. Slice into rounds and place in a greased baking dish.
5. Bake for **20-25 minutes**, then drizzle with extra maple syrup.

Breakfast Quesadilla with Eggs & Salsa

Ingredients:

- 2 eggs, scrambled
- 2 flour tortillas
- 1/2 cup shredded cheese
- 1/4 cup salsa
- 1 tbsp butter

Instructions:

1. Heat butter in a pan and place one tortilla down.
2. Sprinkle with cheese, scrambled eggs, and salsa, then top with another tortilla.
3. Cook until golden brown on both sides.

Eggs Florentine with Spinach & Hollandaise

Ingredients:

- 2 English muffins, toasted
- 2 poached eggs
- 1 cup fresh spinach, sautéed
- 1/2 cup hollandaise sauce

Hollandaise Sauce:

- 3 egg yolks
- 1/2 cup unsalted butter, melted
- 1 tbsp lemon juice
- Salt & cayenne pepper

Instructions:

1. Poach eggs and sauté spinach.
2. Make hollandaise by blending egg yolks, lemon juice, and melted butter.
3. Assemble English muffins with spinach, eggs, and hollandaise.

Peaches & Cream Waffles

Ingredients:

- 2 cups waffle batter (use classic Belgian waffle recipe)
- 1 cup fresh peaches, sliced
- 1/2 cup whipped cream
- 1 tbsp honey

Instructions:

1. Cook waffles in a preheated waffle iron.
2. Top with fresh peaches, whipped cream, and a drizzle of honey.

Biscuits & Country Sausage Gravy

Ingredients:

- 2 cups all-purpose flour
- 1 tbsp baking powder
- 1/2 tsp salt
- 1/2 cup cold butter, cubed
- 3/4 cup milk

Sausage Gravy:

- 1/2 lb breakfast sausage
- 2 tbsp butter
- 2 tbsp flour
- 1 1/2 cups milk
- Salt & black pepper

Instructions:

1. Preheat oven to **400°F (200°C)**. Mix flour, baking powder, and salt.
2. Cut in butter, stir in milk, and form dough. Bake **12-15 minutes**.
3. For gravy, cook sausage, add butter, flour, then whisk in milk.
4. Serve gravy over biscuits.

Hash Brown & Egg Skillet

Ingredients:

- 2 cups shredded hash browns
- 2 eggs
- 1/2 cup shredded cheese
- 1 tbsp butter
- 1 tbsp chopped green onions

Instructions:

1. Cook hash browns in butter until crispy.
2. Make two wells and crack eggs into them.
3. Cover and cook until eggs are set, then sprinkle with cheese and green onions.

Caramelized Banana Oatmeal

Ingredients:

- 1 cup rolled oats
- 2 cups milk or water
- 1 banana, sliced
- 1 tbsp butter
- 1 tbsp brown sugar
- 1/2 tsp cinnamon

Instructions:

1. Cook oats in milk or water.
2. In a skillet, melt butter and cook banana slices with brown sugar and cinnamon until caramelized.
3. Top oatmeal with caramelized bananas.

Creamy Polenta with Poached Eggs

Ingredients:

- 1 cup polenta
- 4 cups water or milk
- 1/2 cup grated Parmesan cheese
- 2 tbsp butter
- 2 poached eggs
- Salt & black pepper

Instructions:

1. Cook polenta in water, stirring for **20 minutes**.
2. Stir in butter, Parmesan, salt, and pepper.
3. Top with poached eggs.

Savory Breakfast Galette with Mushrooms & Goat Cheese

Ingredients:

- 1 sheet puff pastry or homemade dough
- 1/2 cup sautéed mushrooms
- 1/4 cup crumbled goat cheese
- 1 egg yolk (for brushing)
- 1 tsp fresh thyme

Instructions:

1. Preheat oven to **375°F (190°C)**.
2. Roll out pastry, spread mushrooms and goat cheese, and fold edges.
3. Brush with egg yolk and bake for **20-25 minutes**.

Classic Breakfast Muffins with Blueberries

Ingredients:

- 2 cups all-purpose flour
- 1/2 cup sugar
- 2 tsp baking powder
- 1/2 tsp salt
- 1/2 cup milk
- 1/2 cup butter, melted
- 2 eggs
- 1 cup fresh blueberries

Instructions:

1. Preheat oven to **375°F (190°C)**.
2. Mix dry ingredients, then fold in wet ingredients and blueberries.
3. Fill muffin tins and bake for **18-20 minutes**.

Peanut Butter & Banana Smoothie Bowl

Ingredients:

- 1 banana, frozen
- 1/2 cup Greek yogurt
- 1/2 cup almond milk
- 1 tbsp peanut butter
- 1 tbsp chia seeds

Instructions:

1. Blend all ingredients until smooth.
2. Pour into a bowl and top with granola, banana slices, and nuts.

Sweet Potato & Black Bean Breakfast Hash

Ingredients:

- 1 sweet potato, diced
- 1/2 cup black beans
- 1/2 tsp cumin
- 1/2 tsp smoked paprika
- 2 eggs, fried or scrambled
- 1 tbsp chopped cilantro

Instructions:

1. Sauté sweet potatoes in a pan until soft.
2. Add black beans and spices.
3. Serve with eggs and top with cilantro.

Apple Cinnamon Crêpes

Ingredients:

- 1 cup all-purpose flour
- 1 1/4 cups milk
- 2 eggs
- 1 tbsp sugar
- 1 tsp vanilla extract
- 1 apple, thinly sliced
- 1/2 tsp cinnamon
- 1 tbsp honey

Instructions:

1. Blend crepe batter and let rest for **10 minutes**.
2. Cook thin crepes in a buttered pan.
3. Sauté apples with cinnamon and honey, then fill crepes.

Pumpkin Spice Pancakes

Ingredients:

- 1 1/2 cups all-purpose flour
- 1 tbsp sugar
- 1 tsp baking powder
- 1/2 tsp baking soda
- 1/2 tsp salt
- 1/2 tsp pumpkin spice
- 1/2 cup pumpkin purée
- 1 cup milk
- 1 egg
- 2 tbsp melted butter

Instructions:

1. Mix dry and wet ingredients separately, then combine.
2. Cook pancakes on a skillet over medium heat.

Sourdough Toast with Honey & Ricotta

Ingredients:

- 2 slices sourdough bread, toasted
- 1/2 cup ricotta cheese
- 1 tbsp honey
- 1/2 tsp sea salt

Instructions:

1. Spread ricotta on toast.
2. Drizzle with honey and sprinkle with sea salt.

Soft-Boiled Eggs with Toast Soldiers

Ingredients:

- 2 eggs
- 2 slices bread, toasted and cut into strips
- Salt & pepper

Instructions:

1. Boil eggs for **6 minutes**, then transfer to ice water.
2. Peel and serve with toast strips for dipping.

Croque Madame with Gruyère & Ham

Ingredients:

- 2 slices brioche or sourdough bread
- 2 slices ham
- 1/2 cup grated Gruyère cheese
- 1 tbsp Dijon mustard
- 1 tbsp butter
- 1 egg, fried

Instructions:

1. Assemble sandwich with ham, cheese, and Dijon mustard.
2. Butter and toast in a skillet until golden.
3. Top with a fried egg before serving.

Raspberry Almond Danish Pastries

Ingredients:

- 1 sheet puff pastry, thawed
- 1/4 cup raspberry jam
- 1/4 cup fresh raspberries
- 1/4 cup almond paste or frangipane
- 1 egg, beaten (for egg wash)
- 2 tbsp sliced almonds
- Powdered sugar for dusting

Instructions:

1. Preheat oven to **375°F (190°C)**.
2. Cut puff pastry into squares and add a spoonful of almond paste and raspberry jam in the center.
3. Fold into a pinwheel or leave open, brushing edges with egg wash.
4. Bake for **15-18 minutes**, then sprinkle with sliced almonds and dust with powdered sugar.

Green Smoothie Bowl with Granola

Ingredients:

- 1 frozen banana
- 1/2 cup spinach or kale
- 1/2 cup almond milk
- 1 tbsp chia seeds
- 1/2 cup granola (for topping)

Instructions:

1. Blend all ingredients until smooth.
2. Pour into a bowl and top with granola, fresh fruit, and seeds.

Classic Breakfast Quiche with Bacon & Spinach

Ingredients:

- 1 pie crust
- 6 eggs
- 1 cup milk
- 1/2 cup cooked bacon, crumbled
- 1/2 cup fresh spinach, chopped
- 1/2 cup shredded Gruyère or cheddar cheese
- Salt & pepper to taste

Instructions:

1. Preheat oven to **375°F (190°C)**.
2. Whisk eggs, milk, salt, and pepper.
3. Layer bacon, spinach, and cheese in pie crust.
4. Pour egg mixture over and bake for **35-40 minutes**.

Granola & Greek Yogurt with Honey

Ingredients:

- 1 cup Greek yogurt
- 1/2 cup granola
- 1 tbsp honey

Instructions:

1. Layer yogurt and granola in a bowl.
2. Drizzle with honey and add fresh fruit if desired.

Chocolate Chip Muffins with Espresso

Ingredients:

- 2 cups all-purpose flour
- 1/2 cup sugar
- 1 tbsp baking powder
- 1/2 tsp salt
- 1/2 cup milk
- 1/4 cup strong brewed espresso
- 1/2 cup melted butter
- 2 eggs
- 1 cup chocolate chips

Instructions:

1. Preheat oven to **375°F (190°C)**.
2. Mix dry ingredients, then fold in wet ingredients and chocolate chips.
3. Fill muffin tins and bake for **18-20 minutes**.

Coconut Chia Pudding with Mango

Ingredients:

- 1/4 cup chia seeds
- 1 cup coconut milk
- 1 tbsp honey
- 1/2 cup diced mango

Instructions:

1. Mix chia seeds, coconut milk, and honey.
2. Refrigerate overnight, then top with mango before serving.

Carrot Cake Waffles with Cream Cheese Drizzle

Ingredients:

- 1 cup all-purpose flour
- 1/2 cup shredded carrots
- 1/2 tsp cinnamon
- 1/4 tsp nutmeg
- 1/2 cup milk
- 1 egg
- 2 tbsp melted butter

Cream Cheese Drizzle:

- 2 tbsp cream cheese
- 1 tbsp honey
- 1 tbsp milk

Instructions:

1. Mix waffle ingredients and cook in a preheated waffle iron.
2. Mix cream cheese drizzle and pour over waffles.

Vanilla Bean Porridge with Roasted Nuts

Ingredients:

- 1 cup rolled oats
- 2 cups milk or water
- 1 tsp vanilla bean paste
- 1 tbsp honey
- 1/4 cup roasted nuts (almonds, pecans, or walnuts)

Instructions:

1. Cook oats in milk or water.
2. Stir in vanilla bean paste and honey.
3. Top with roasted nuts.

Cheesy Grits with Butter & Shrimp

Ingredients:

- 1 cup stone-ground grits
- 4 cups water or milk
- 1 cup shredded cheddar cheese
- 1 tbsp butter
- 1/2 lb shrimp, cooked
- 1/2 tsp paprika

Instructions:

1. Cook grits in water/milk, stirring until thick.
2. Stir in butter and cheese.
3. Serve with sautéed shrimp and paprika.

Mocha Smoothie with Almond Butter

Ingredients:

- 1 frozen banana
- 1/2 cup cold brewed coffee
- 1/2 cup almond milk
- 1 tbsp cocoa powder
- 1 tbsp almond butter

Instructions:

1. Blend all ingredients until smooth.
2. Serve immediately with ice if desired.

Freshly Baked Pain au Chocolat

Ingredients:

- 1 sheet puff pastry
- 2 oz dark chocolate, chopped
- 1 egg, beaten (for egg wash)

Instructions:

1. Preheat oven to **375°F (190°C)**.
2. Cut puff pastry into rectangles, place chocolate in the center, and fold over.
3. Brush with egg wash and bake for **15-18 minutes**.